Beautiful
Wyoming

Beautiful
Wyoming

Concept and Design: Robert D. Shangle
Text: Brian Berger

First Printing June, 1980
Published by Beautiful America Publishing Company
P.O. Box 608, Beaverton, Oregon 97075
Robert D. Shangle, Publisher

Library of Congress Cataloging in Publication Data
Beautiful Wyoming
1. Wyoming—Description and travel—Views. I. Title.
F762.B47   917.87'0022'2   79-25372
ISBN 0-89802-094-8
ISBN 0-89802-093-X (paperback)

Photo Credits

Contents

Introduction

"At last, the wide sky, the wide land . . . stretching
far to the limitless blue sky of Wyoming. Room to
breathe, to stretch one's soul's wings again. Here
the big country still is."

Margaret & Olaus Murie
Wapiti Wilderness

The writings of Wyoming's early diarists, novelists, and journalists are filled with awed and whimsical observations of the state's spaciousness. This is little wonder, for Wyoming, with an area of 97,914 square miles, is our ninth largest state; a land that challenges the senses to encompass its total beauty. To 375,000 Wyomingites, it is a land of beauty in the extreme: from the vastness of the Great Divide Basin country, where the early westbound emigrants experienced the hardships of an arid terrain, to the extreme heights of the magnificent Teton Range, overlooking the southern portions of the state's famous Yellowstone Park.

Since Wyoming's acquisition as part of the Louisiana Purchase in 1803, the state has never had more than eight percent of its soil subjected to the plow. This fact has led one historian to note that, "No one wanted to live in Wyoming—they just wanted to pass over the ground because it led somewhere else." Bill Nye (an early Wyoming journalist), jesting about the state's farm produce in one of his editorials, said: "Unless the yield this fall of moss agates and prickly pears should be unusually large, the agricultural export will be far below preceding years, and there may be actual suffering." Kidding aside, old Bill Nye, when he wasn't poking fun at Wyoming's land or weather, was probably enthralled by the grandeur of the state's diverse landforms, and invigorated by its climate.

It was Wyoming's austere portions that first greeted the early emigrants who sought to cross the state's southern expanse. This area gave rise to the notion that Wyoming was nothing but a "Great Desert." And there is desert here. So much of it, that Wyoming's arid and semi-arid regions comprise more than half of the state's total area. Where the land rises to the foothills, there are endless vistas of low sagebrush, prickly pear, and greasewood, mixing with juniper and mountain mahogany. Where rivers cleave through this brush country, their moist banks support box elder and peach-leafed willow. Near the land's interior are great plains of grassland, sprouting blue grama, June grass, wheat and needle grasses. Mixing with these are saltsage, vetch, and alkali spike grasses. Feeding on this assortment of ground cover, or hiding under it from predators lurking nearby, are mule deer and pronghorn antelope, as well as the lightning-fast prairie dog and the camouflaged sage grouse. Here, too, are the quick-paced ground squirrel and pocket gopher, ever watchful for the circlings of the prairie falcon.

As one leaves these drier surroundings and enters the mountainous terrain of Wyoming's northwestern sections, the vegetation becomes thicker and the mountains, asserting their ruggedness, sharply display a contrast against the distant plains. These are not just mountains; these are towering perpendicular walls of heart-stopping immenseness. Here, one can watch the never-tiring display of the seasons, contrasting against their craggy bulk. The mountains, highlighted by burnished golds from the rays of a setting sun, glisten with a dusk-filtered pinkness as the great drama that is a Wyoming day fades against their icy pinnacles.

When autumn touches this land, the valleys take on the dappled richness of summer's passing. Leaves of bright yellow, subdued tangerine and hectic red mix with the more subtle shades of emerald and the dark green of pine. In the winter, if one is positioned right, the icy-blueness of a partly frozen Snake River can be seen, its serpentine meanderings fronting the greater spectacle of the Tetons.

Few natural wonders can equal the display of the Tetons' rugged might. These mountains compel one to face their stately presence. They stand as the work of some primal force, seeming even now to be reaching ever higher against a cobalt sky. The jagged faces of these mountains, when covered by winter snows, radiates a cold majesty that is humbling. Thoughts are turned to the power of the earth-shaping forces that created them. When the land has taken on an icy crispness, dusted by a thin blanket of new snow, one is made to stand silent, entranced, before the scene's magnitude of crystalline surroundings.

Farther north lies the scenic marvel that is Yellowstone National Park. Here one will marvel at the colorful sinter mounds of Mammoth Hot Springs, the steaming, emerald basin of Grand Prismatic Spring, and the eruptive displays of the park's boiling geysers. This area has been referred to at various times as *Colter's Hell*, named after John Colter, the first white man to see the Yellowstone geysers. It may be more accurately described as "probably the greatest laboratory that nature furnishes on the surface of the globe." The park offers the visitor a unique visual experience. A chance to experience the unparalleled beauty of 2¼-million acres of wilderness is there for the taking.

Beautiful Wyoming is more than the sum of its bold and sweeping topography: it is the history of westward expansion. Played across Wyoming's landscape was the drama of white man against red man, of mountain man against the forces of nature, and of settlers against the state's vast and arid vistas. Wyoming is an important part of the history that shaped this nation. It holds for the visitor vast open spaces and historically rich towns. It offers a chance to immerse oneself in much the same environment that confronted early explorers and hardy settlers of the land.

Brian Berger

The Way West

"It was a wild, strong sight, a rich and powerful sight
that awed a man and lifted him inside—the plains climbing into ridges where, once in a long while, trees stood
spare and tough, the sky curved across, so blue it pained
the eye, far things brought close and sharp as through
a glass, and buffalo on all the land and the roll of their
bellowing in all the air."

A.B. Guthrie, Jr.
The Way West

Much of Wyoming's history deals in great part with the story of the westward movement. For the emigrants, who chose the state's central portions as their pathway to the lands of plenty farther west, it was a story of high hopes dwindling to disillusionment and of severe hardships overcome by dogged perserverance.

The path these stalwart individuals chose to follow in their quest for fertile lands, a temperate climate, and fabled riches is best known today as the Oregon Trail. The name is somewhat misleading, for most who traveled the trail were, in fact, not headed for Oregon. Many sought instead the golden lands of California, while others made Utah their final destination. It was during their journey through this mostly arid central section of Wyoming, that many a frustrated and weary emigrant decided that this land was nothing more than a part of the "Great American Desert." The best said about it was "Sand, sand, sand!" Yet despite the hardships, Wyoming's section of the trail, known also as The Great Platte River Road, became the "super highway" of westward expansion. Between 1841 and 1868, more than 400,000 expansionists would cross the trail's harsh terrain.

Visitors, wishing to trace the footsteps of the hardy pioneers, will find themselves traveling through five of central Wyoming's counties: Goshen, Platte, Converse, Natrona, and Fremont. The first of these, Goshen County, is an area of rich croplands, growing an abundance of wheat, sugar beets, potatoes, drybeans, corn, and hay. There are few towns in this region of productive farmlands. But one,

Fort Laramie, has an adjacent garrison (Fort Laramie National Historic Site) that was considered a major gathering spot for emigrants entering southeastern Wyoming. Twenty-two original structures occupy the fort's grounds, oldest of which is Old Bedlam built in 1849, and erected when the one-time trapping outpost was taken over by the Army. Since 1938, when 214 acres of this former military reservation land was proclaimed a National Monument, thousands have visited what was once a way-station for gold seekers, tired emigrants, the Pony Express, and the Overland Stage.

Platte County's 2,086 square miles of irrigated farmlands greet the trail follower next. The Platte River Road winds through the north-central section of this county, rougher portions of which are pock-marked by the early efforts of prospectors. Located just south of the town of Guernsey is Register Cliff, a popular overnight campsite for emigrants having traveled one day's journey out of Fort Laramie. It is one of the most notable county tourist attractions. The cliff bears the carved names and the dates of passage of many of those who stopped here. Nearby, the actual trail-ruts made by the wheels of the emigrants heavily-loaded wagons appear today, almost exactly as they did to the pioneer wagonmasters.

The town of Glendo lies along the western shore of Glendo Reservoir. Known early on as the Old Horseshoe Stage Station, the town was a stopping point for the Pony Express. From here, Glendo Lake State Park is a four-mile drive east. A popular water sports area, the 12,500-acre lake is famous for year-round walleye and trout fishing. Overnight accommodations are available along the lake's shores, as well as complete camping facilities and day-use areas.

Crossing into Converse County, one enters the ninth largest of Wyoming's counties. The smooth path of Interstate 25 (a far cry from the rutted trail the pioneers negotiated) allows for quick travel between the county's major towns. Douglas, the largest town, is the county seat. Settled in 1886, within a few days after rumors of the railroads intention to build in the area was confirmed, Douglas soon became an important shipping point for cattle. Its importance was short-lived. A severe winter in 1887 brought death to many cattle. By 1890, agriculture was fast replacing livestock as Douglas' economic base. It remains so today.

Douglas is host to the annual Wyoming State Fair, an event which has taken place in August of each year since 1905. Also of interest for the tourist is a trip to the town's center to view the only replica (so the town's residents claim) of the most rare of North American animals—the Jackalope. Looking part jackrabbit and part pronghorn antelope, the statue is said to be exact in every detail, being modeled after a rare mounted specimen. It is said the specimen is so rare that no one can recall ever having seen it. But that doesn't seem to matter to the town's citizens, as they enthusiastically explain its habits to passing tourists.

Natrona County's major city, and the second largest in Wyoming, is Casper. Centrally located within the state, Casper acts as a hub from which a visitor can quickly reach many points of historic interest by way of the major arterials that radiate from its heart. The city is an outgrowth of Fort Caspar, an Army headquarters for soldiers who offered protection to wagon trains passing through this area. Through an error in spelling, early records listed the town as Cas*per*, rather than Cas*par*, and the error was left uncorrected. Today, the city is the center of the oil and gas industry for the Rocky Mountain region. Four interstate pipelines feed the black gold to a thirsty and demanding public, while most of the major oil companies have established offices in the county to further explore for untapped petroleum fields.

State Highway 220 out of Casper follows the North Platte River to where it crosses the Sweetwater River, nearly paralleling the route of the emigrants. Here, the wagon trains passed by Independence Rock as they sought to traverse the Continental Divide Basin, a 100-mile break in the great Rocky Mountain Barrier. Most settlers found the route to be monotonous; there was little else but sand and sagebrush to entertain them during the nearly five-week journey required to cross the Basin's vast sandy spaces. That this stretch of the journey took its toll in lives can be seen by the many graves that line the route. Some died as infants, unable to cope with the land's harshness; others, by the emigrants most common ailments, cholera and dysentery

The inscriptions of many of the travelers who later died along this route can be seen where they carved them, in the huge granite dome that is Independence Rock. Located 50 miles southwest of Casper, Independence Rock sits on a flat landscape, its smooth granite dome having the appearance of a great turtle shell. Covering some 27 acres, the dome rises 193 feet above the valley floor. More than 5,000 names cover the gray rock's expanse: those of explorers, trappers, missionaries, and emigrants. Unknowingly, some carved their own epitaphs only weeks before they fell victim to the land's unforgiving nature.

Five miles southwest of Independence Rock is Devil's Gate, a deep gorge cut through the Rattlesnake Mountains by the Sweetwater River. Devil's Gate seems to be the work of an early-day road crew, who, in anticipation of the westward movement, had been busily clearing away some of the formidable obstacles in the emigrants path. For some 400 yards the Sweetwater has eroded its way through solid granite, to leave a natural cut with nearly perpendicular 350-foot walls.

From Devil's Gate, the emigrants were faced with a gradual climb for another 60 miles, over a very rocky and mountainous road, to the broad plain on the Continental Divide known as South Pass. The gain in elevation to the summit of this flat space on the "backbone of the Rockies" went unnoticed. The only way the emigrants could tell they had crossed the Divide was to note that the water now flowed in a westerly direction.

A short distance northeast of South Pass, on Willow Creek just off Wyoming Highway 28, is the townsite of South Pass City. The town was built in the fall of 1867, during the rush for gold that was found in the area. The town's one-time population of 2,000, made up mostly of prospectors, has dwindled to about a dozen residents.

Recreation in Fremont County is varied and plentiful. Three National Forests lie partly within its boundaries: Bridger, Shoshone, and Teton. Mule deer, elk, and bighorn sheep are plentiful within these areas, making hunting one of the region's most popular sports. Fishing is a favorite pastime for visitors with public easements being maintained by the Fish and Game Department along Wind River, Jakey's Fork in the Dubois area, and a number of rivers in the Lander area. Dude ranches can be found throughout the county. A visitor will find them a good base for rockhunting, hiking, camping, or just picnicking. In the winter, activities include cross-country skiing, snowmobiling, and ice fishing.

The story of the Oregon Trail is indeed one of the most colorful chapters of Wyoming's history. Though changed in spots by the growth of a few large cities, essentially the trail appears the same as when the first emigrants tested themselves against its hardships. For the visitor who wants to retrace the journey of the emigrants, along this historical pathway carved by the wheels and footprints of a people set on fulfilling their desired goals, it is a rare chance to observe first hand a preserved portion of Wyoming's history.

Homes on the Range

Economically, and populace-wise, the Wyoming of the 1860s owed much to the Union Pacific Railroad's rush to complete a Transcontinental route through the Territory. The growth of many of Wyoming's towns followed the construction of the railroad's tracks, as the iron rails were stretched to join with the Central Pacific's at Promontory Summit, Utah. Forts grew into towns, and other towns emerged from patches of sage. Towns, with now familiar names like Cheyenne, Laramie, Rawlins, Rock Springs, Green River, and Evanston, dotted the railroad's winding course from east to west as it crossed the southern face of the Territory.

With the final joining of the two rail systems, the people that had been drawn to the area to accommodate the railroad workers, and the railroad workers themselves, left the Great Desert for more promising environments. A post-railroad population of some 16,000 dwindled to half that figure. There was need for an economic shot in the arm to stimulate additional growth in the region.

For a brief spell gold looked like it would be that needed boost, with the discovery of ''color'' at South Pass in 1867. But the anticipated boom turned to a bust when the quality of the find proved disappointing. Another discovery of the yellow stuff in the Black Hills some years later proved more rewarding. The miners took sizeable quantities of gold from underground vaults in the hills, well into the 1880s. It was this fevered assault for gold in the northeastern sectors of Wyoming that precipitated the final removal of the state's Indians from their treaty lands.

Wyoming's greatest hope for financial well-being had long centered on coal production. Because of the conniving by railroad officials and strikes by workers against low wages, growth was slow in coming.

Eventually, it was the grassy wealth of Wyoming's vast rangelands, left after the near extinction of the great buffalo herds by the mid-1870s, that would turn the cattle business into an economic force. Great herds were driven from Oregon and Texas to graze, mostly unattended until market time. Even the great spaces of open range became overgrazed because of mismanagement. In the winter of 1886, nearly

400,000 cattle died. Still, livestock dwarfed all other economic activities during the 1880s, and Wyoming's towns were feeling the impact of that wealth.

Cheyenne, the largest of Wyoming's cities, grew rapidly after the rails had reached its doorstep. The town became a haunt of wicked characters looking for quick riches and professional gunmen wanting to enhance their reputations. Today the city depends on the cattle and sheep market for part of its livelihood, together with timber, oil, coal, and the booming tourist business. In July, Cheyenne relives some of the glamour of its beginnings as a cattle empire, by holding the annual Frontier Days Rodeo. Thousands gather at the town's Frontier Park Arena to watch the cream of the nation's broncbusters and bulldoggers compete for the top-prize money. The festivities last for nine days, with a full schedule of activities—pancake breakfasts to late-evening square dancing.

Laramie's early history parallels much of Cheyenne's. The law in towns like Laramie was almost nonexistent. A man known to have committed some misdeed often fell victim to late night visitors—vigilantes. One can form a more vivid picture of the way the town's early inhabitants lived by a visit to the Laramie Plains Museum, which houses an interesting display of period furnishings.

For the ski buff, Medicine Bow Ski Area, about a 45-minute drive west of Laramie, offers snowy recreation and a chance to enjoy the magnificent scenery of the surrounding national forest.

For those young cowpokes hoping to make future headlines at Cheyenne's big rodeo, the Little Britches Rodeo, held in July at the town of Rawlins, is open to youngsters under 18 years of age. It is every bit as lively as the bigger show. Seminoe Lake Park lies just northeast of the town, where giant sand dunes enclose a sparkling lake full of trout. Here, too, thousands of pronghorn antelope find refuge in the park's acres of sagebrush.

Thunder Basin National Grassland's is located between the cities of Casper and Sundance, covering nearly two-million acres of partly redeemed grazing lands. Homesteaders who came to this region, armed only with knowledge of the farming methods that had worked for them in moister climates, over-estimated the numbers of stock that could be accommodated on their small tracts of land. It quickly turned the Basin into a ''dust bowl'' area. Today, proper management has again allowed large herds of cattle and sheep, along with one of the world's largest herds of pronghorn antelope, to graze contentedly on portions of these recovered lands.

Sundance, located in the Black Hills of northeastern Wyoming, is surrounded by a number of ghost towns that owed their previous existence to the discovery of gold in the area. In the summer months, the town's population swells with visitors hoping to camp in Black Hills National Forest, or on their way to view the nation's first national monument, Devil's Tower. Looking like the petrified remains of a giant, ancient tree trunk, Devil's Tower rears its fluted, nearly vertical wall 1,280 feet above the Belle Fourche Valley. A massive upwelling of molten rock, which gradually cooled and crystallized, formed this tallest rock formation of its kind in the United States, some 50 million years ago. The Indians of the region have their own story of how the tower's polygonal columns were formed. They say the deep scars resulted from the sharp claws of a huge bear that had attempted to catch an Indian maiden, but was thwarted in its efforts by a platform that rose from the landscape, saving her from the bear's grasp.

Standing magnificent amid the surroundings of Wyoming's north-central section is the Bighorn Mountain Range, home of the Bighorn National Forest which covers 1,121,541 acres of mountainous terrain. There are excellent hunting, camping, and fishing grounds here. One will find a large number of mule deer sharing the rich forests and meadows with nearly 4,000 elk, and a small herd of bighorn sheep. Many small towns edge the borders of the Bighorn wilderness, a number of them having colorful frontier names: Big Horn, Buffalo, Big Trails, Greybull, and Ten Sleep. Ten Sleep was named by the Indians for the time needed to reach it from Fort Laramie. The region's largest city, Sheridan, like Cheyenne is another famed rodeo center. In mid-July, the Sheridan Wyoming Rodeo draws the nation's top professional cowboys.

The city of Cody, named for William F. Cody, better known as Buffalo Bill, borders the eastern slopes of the Absaroka Mountain Range. Cody is steeped in the lore of Wyoming's early days. Much of the personal memorabilia of the famed frontiersman is housed in the town's Buffalo Bill Historical Center. Three other collections are housed at the Center also: the Whitney Gallery of Western Art, the Plains Indians Museum, and the Winchester Gun Museum. The center is the perfect place to trace Wyoming's frontier beginnings, displaying original documents, photographs, paintings, and the weapons and costumes of settlers and Indians.

West of Cody is another huge wilderness area, the Shoshone National Forest. Abundant with wildlife, the forest's 2½-million acres of lofty pine and spruce carpet one of the country's largest national forests with their greenery. Outstanding resorts and dude ranches dot the area, offering comfortable places from which to explore this vast timber reserve, sparkling here and there with the blue and silver waters of icy lakes and streams.

Bypassing the great wilderness that is the Yellowstone, one might next visit the city of Jackson, located near the mighty Tetons. The city is the perfect launching point for enjoying the unlimited recreational pleasures to be found in the 400-square-mile valley that is Jackson Hole. A haven for elk, moose, antelope, and bighorn sheep, the valley is also a lure for thousands of fishermen who are challenged by the trophy-sized trout found in its lakes and streams. High on the slopes of the Jackson Hole Ski Area, downhill ski enthusiasts will have a commanding view of the surroundings, finding the scene breathtaking as they make their way to the bottom of a 4,000-foot slope, to again be chair-lifted to the powdery playground.

Previous page: Square Top Peak in the Wind River Mountains
Opposite: Grand Teton National Park
Above: Gardner River in Yellowstone National Park

19

Above: Grand Teton National Park
Opposite: Chimney Rock at Shell Canyon

Above: Near Sundance on the way to Devil's Tower
Opposite: Teewinot Mountain in the Grand Tetons
Following pages: The Snake River and the Grand Tetons

22

Opposite: Autumn in the Grand Tetons
Above: Geyser Basin at West Thumb in Yellowstone National Park

27

Opposite: A Wyoming Bighorn Sheep
Above: The St. John mountain group in the Teton Range

29

Above: Red Creek Badlands in southwest Wyoming
Opposite: Minerva Terrace in Mammoth Hot Springs,
Yellowstone National Park.

Opposite: Belle Fourche River in Devil's Tower National Monument
Above: Shell Canyon and Shell Creek

33

Opposite: Shell Canyon
Above: Old Faithful

35

Previous page: Grand Teton National Park
Above: The Tetons and Gros Ventre River
Opposite: Balsam root and lupine

Opposite: An autumn scene northeast of Jackson
Above: Medicine Bow Peak

41

Opposite: Natural Bridge at Ayres Park
Above: Wind River Canyon

43

Above: The Mormon Trail
Opposite: Mt. Moran reflected in the Snake River

Above: Chapel of the Transfiguration, Grand Teton National Park
Opposite: Windmill near Casper
Following page: Yellowstone Falls

46

Previous page: Grand Teton National Park
Above: Hills near Dubois
Opposite: Thermopolis Hot Mineral Springs

50

Above: Bighorn Forest
Opposite: Pinnacle Buttes and Brooks Lake, Shoshone National Forest

Opposite: Lake Marie, Medicine Bow Mountains
Above: Independence Rock
Following pages: Devil's Tower

Above: An old trail town in Cody
Opposite: Officers Quarters at Fort Laramie

Opposite: Grand Teton National Park
Above: An elk in Yellowstone National Park

Opposite: Devil's Gate and the Sweetwater River
Above: A field of wildflowers near Powder River Pass
Following page: Autumn along Jenny Lake in the Grand Teton National Park

The Tetons

"... [Past] the wide desert scene of Wyoming . . .
the land rises and climbs as you go westward, and there
is another world, a mountain world of very special and
extraordinary beauty . . . . Man is here, but he has not
yet laid a heavy hand on his surroundings."

Wapiti Wilderness

Wyoming is truly the land of greatness. The ruggedness of her mountainous terrain and the vastness of her arid plains seems to have forestalled the encroachment of man from marring the state's abundance of natural beauty. And nowhere on Wyoming's landscape is her beauty better exemplified than in the ice and wind sculptured ruggedness of the Teton Range.

Envision an almost flat volcanic plateau. The warm seas that once covered most of North America have drained away, due to the gradual uplifting of their flooring. Fissures in the earth's crust have allowed molten rock to ooze out upon the land, cooling and forming an igneous pavement over great portions of the continent. Deep beneath the land's surface, immense pressures building against rocky layers suddenly release the energy of ages in a massive rending of the earth's crust, thrusting the underlying rock skyward. So clean is the upthrust of the land's eastern face, it seems as if a giant rock wall has risen from the depths of the flattened landscape. Where the wall has tilted to the west, the contrast of flat land to newly formed mountains is not as abrupt, but instead, it slopes gently into the landscape. These are the Tetons, known to the Indians as "Teewinot."

The Tetons *then*, were not the Tetons as we know them today. It would be tens of thousands of years before the Indians of the region would label these mountains, now weathered and glaciated, Teewinot, meaning "many peaks." These mighty peaks are surely what mountains were meant to look like: a monumental exhibit of the earth's raw energy, unleashed against its own constraining forces.

It is known that there are still mountain-forming forces actively at work beneath the Teton Range, as indicated by signs of fault movement within the last three thousand years. Although the Tetons are considered a young mountain range—that is, in geological time—it is amazing to find that parts of its rocky structure have been given age datings of 2½ billion years. What profound changes in the earth's face have taken place within this incomprehensible time span can only be guessed. It is believed that the formation of the Tetons is part of an endless earth-shaping cycle that, eventually, will reduce their bulk to featureless landscape, and then, once again mountains will arise.

When first viewing the delights of Grand Teton National Park, a visitor is immediately overwhelmed by the dominating outlines of the Tetons rugged peaks, cleaving to the cold air mass more than a mile above the Wyoming landscape. One will note the deep, jagged scars left by the eroding processes of wind-driven rains, and the accompanying torrents of water that chewed through solid rock in descending to the land below. One will see where massive glaciers carved gigantic chunks from the Tetons steep faces, leaving ragged grooves of shadow-catching deepness. In their descent to the very base of these mountains, massive ice packs bulldozed piles of rock debris, helping to form the basins for the park's lakes.

While viewing the rich expanse of pine spreading out from the base of the Tetons, where the gleaming Snake River mirrors the trees in rippling green patterns, one will perhaps feel the same awe that overcame the first white man to marvel at the Teton's chiseled might—John Colter. A fur trapper of uncommon endurance, Colter passed through the Jackson Hole, Teton, and Yellowstone wilderness in 1807. He was the first to tell of the land's many wonders. Understandably, Colter had a difficult time convincing anyone that he had really seen these magnificent sights, especially when describing the geyser activity of Yellowstone. Eventually many came to find this land much as Colter described it, and thereafter returned with their own glowing tales of its beauty.

Today, another type of explorer is still finding Teton National Park a land to talk about. He doesn't come on foot, wearing the moccasins of a mountain man, but instead, covers great distances in shiny machines, reaching the park's primal spaces in a matter of hours. So that none can dispute his claim to the enchanting lands he has seen, he carries other machines that record the unrivaled grandeur that is everywhere within the park's boundaries. But most importantly, he may take home with him something that vehicles cannot reach and cameras cannot capture—a better understanding of the essence of what wilderness once was.

Perhaps one is first aware of a feeling of primal beauty created by the Teton's subtle moods when night closes about the highest of the snow-covered peaks. Or perhaps the feeling is prompted by the biting chill of the park's early morning air, as one watches low-lying clouds slowly dissipate, unveiling the gilt-lined shadow areas of the Teton's steep faces. Whatever the reason for a visitor's growing awareness of the qualities that make the Teton wilderness area unique, it will be a lasting impression that, in the end, will ensure the continued protection of our nation's national parks.

The Yellowstone

The year was 1807. Emerging from the forests of the Teton wilderness, a lone figure surveyed his surroundings and quietly re-entered the pine-canopied darkness. Limping slightly, he shrugged off the recurrent pain of a deep leg wound (the result of a fight with Indians) and headed in the direction of the Yellowstone. The man was John Colter, one of the tough breed of mountain men who made their living trapping beaver, mink, and otter on the unexplored rivers of the western territories. With his friends the Crow Indians, Colter had tangled with a party of Blackfeet. Escaping into the forest he was now headed north-eastward, away from the area of Jackson Hole, to his camp at the fort on the shores of the Bighorn River.

Colter arrived safely. It is believed that his journey had taken him through what is now the nation's first and largest national park—Yellowstone. Colter related tales of ''earth-trembling . . . seething infernos, [and] boiling waters that erupt into millions of tiny cascading diamonds.'' Much later, another trapper, Jim Bridger, described seeing ''a column of water as big around as my body spouting 60 feet in the air.'' Then, as if to top his own tall-tale, he told of ''a mountain of transparent glass'' (Obsidian Cliff) that, when viewed through, made distant things appear close—so close that Bridger wasted a number of shots at an elk before he realized that the mountain was magnifying its image from miles away. It is easy to understand why people had a hard time believing him, for he loved to embellish on the truth.

Embellishment or not, most of today's Yellowstone visitors will find these early tales to be nearly accurate (the magnifying mountain aside). What they will see are the park's famed geysers spewing steaming columns of water on a nearly predictable recurring schedule. Old Faithful seems to be the most popular. Visitors can view Yellowstone's Grand Prismatic Spring, a 370-foot-wide pool of steaming emerald water, situated within a setting of umber and yellow algae, or marvel at the frosted terraces of Mammoth Hot Springs, built up from deposits of mineral-rich waters. For those who would relinquish the home-away-from-home conveniences of their travel trailers, the grandeur of Yellowstone's back-country beckons. Here is an area that fewer than five percent of the park's visitors ever see. It is a land that can test the stamina of even the experienced hiker, while rewarding him lavishly for every ounce of the effort.

Near Specimen Ridge, in the park's northeastern section, lies the petrified remains of an ancient forest. Here, one can trek through 40 square miles of woods that has turned to rock. Once a forest of towering oak, redwood, pine, and hickory, these giants now lie scattered atop 27 layers of yet more ancient forests. Southwest of Specimen Ridge, the Yellowstone River cascades over Lower Falls in the park's Grand Canyon area, plunging 308 feet into the mist-shrouded river below.

The backpacker will not want to miss the view from Two Ocean Plateau, where one can see great portions of the Absaroka Mountain Range, its trailing Wind River Range, the Tetons, and the pristine waters of Yellowstone Lake. The largest body of water in the park, Yellowstone Lake takes its name (as does the park itself) from the waters of the Yellowstone River. Given the name *Mi tsi a-da-zi* by the Minnetaree Indians, the river's name translates as ''Yellow Rock River.'' One of Yellowstone's early explorers, Ferdinand V. Hayden said of the lake: ''[It is] a vast sheet of quiet water . . . one of the most beautiful scenes I have ever beheld . . . such a vision is worth a lifetime, and only one of such beauty will ever greet human eyes.''

And from the journal of Pitt Langford (organizer of the Washburn expedition of 1870): ''We came to camp on the shores of Yellowstone Lake. Today the winds lash it into a raging sea covered with foam, while the sparkling sand along the shore seems to form a jewelled setting. Water never seemed so beautiful before.''

To view the lake's many moods is to understand the excitement of its early spokesmen. Covering a great portion of the park's south-eastern section, the waters spread over an area of 136 miles, reaching an average depth of 139 feet. It has been said that Yellowstone Lake holds one of the most perfectly functioning aquatic communities remaining on the continent. What is more amazing is its fish population: the lake is known to contain only one kind of trout, the cutthroat. Its food source, the freshwater shrimp, is here in such quantities that estimates have placed the cutthroat population in the millions, due to the abundance of their favorite meal.

Adding to the comfort of a visitor's stay are the excellent accommodations fronting the lake's shores. Boats can be rented at Bridge Bay and Grant Village or the navigation of its waters can be left to the captain of the ''Scenicruiser,'' while a visitor enjoys the sights around Stevenson Island. Considered to be one of the best fishing spots in all of Wyoming, Yellowstone Lake is also frequented by non-human fishermen. The pelican population may consume as many as half-a-million cutthroat annually, while the cormorants, terns, kingfishers, and herons contribute their ravenous appetites to controlling the cutthroats proliferation.

Two other bodies of water can be viewed from the upper portion of the park's Pichstone Plateau—Shoshone and Lewis Lakes. The plateau was formed when taffy-like lava flows were squeezed into pressure ridges, creating a surface that, as one *National Geographic* writer noted, "seems a moonscape with frozen waves of black sand." Many of the park's streams obtain their waters from high plateaus like Pichstone. They wind their way through dense forests of Lodgepole pine and lush meadows, finally to join larger rivers or feed into mirror-like lakes. Pichstone is curiously devoid of heavy growth, but does exhibit colorful fields of the reddish-purple little red elephant flower. Elsewhere along the path, leading from Pichstone, blue lupine mingle with red Indian paintbrush and the air is scented with the pungent smell of the surrounding pine.

Perhaps the most awesome display of the seething forces that still underlie the greenness of Yellowstone is its geysers. Once having witnessed their steaming eruptions, one will understand why they named Yellowstone *Colter's Hell*. The underlying causes for this display of boiling hostility are found thousands of feet underground, where surface waters have seeped into layers of hot rock. The oven-like temperatures of these rocks heat the underground waters to nearly 400-degrees fahrenheit, causing pressures which force the liquid to the surface and create the spectacular geysers that Yellowstone is famous for. Where steam pressures are not great enough to force the ascending waters into the familiar geyser form, their slow escape produces the hot springs of this region. Mammoth Hot Springs, near park headquarters, is generally singled out as the crowning effort of these mineral-rich waters. Here the steady flow of waters, welling up through deep layers of limestone, have built terraces of softly-shaded purple and brown tones, coated delicately with frosty-white calcium carbonate.

Yellowstone has an abundance of wildlife. Though the footprints of the wolf and mountain lion have nearly disappeared due to early trapping efforts, the park is still home for about 200 grizzly bear and 400 black bear. Also finding a refuge here are large herds of elk (at times needing to be thinned out because of an overgrazing problem) and smaller herds of moose, bighorn sheep, and bison. Of the smaller animals one is likely to encounter, perhaps the most prevalent is the ever-inquisitive squirrel, chattering at the intrusion into his private dining preserve. Almost as inquisitive is his cousin the chipmunk, occasionally seen scurrying across the trail only yards ahead of unexpected visitors. Circling the skies are the ever-vigilant hawks, and the occasional golden eagle, hoping to snag the unwary gopher or snowshoe hare. When night settles across the Yellowstone, one is apt to hear the most vocal of the park's predators, the coyote, singing to the blackened depths of a star-bejewelled sky.

Although the likelihood of a bear attack is minimal, the backpacker would be well advised to take a few precautions while treking through *Ursus horribilis'* backyard. Foremost would be to keep food scraps from around the campsite and place any foodstuffs at a fair distance from one's sleeping area. Secondly, pitching one's tent near a good climbing tree, while not essential, can do a lot for the nerves if that imagined shagginess in the shadows turns out to be the real thing.

Hiking, fishing, camping, or just sightseeing, Yellowstone offers the summer visitor plenty of exciting, informative activities. But, for the visitor who would travel to this national wonderland in winter, the park displays a unique beauty that is missed by the fair-weather crowd. The trees near the geysers are veiled in the frozen vapors of their steaming eruptions. The land glistens with a blue-white radiance, as the sun reflects off of its frosty surface. For those who would test their stamina on Yellowstone's back-country trails, snowshoes provide a way to melt into the quiet of the distant landscape. Here, nestled in Yellowstone's snow-blanketed vastness, the modern explorer will rediscover the beauty that captivated those who first treked the park's frozen wilderness: a beauty that prompted the preservation of Yellowstone's splendid topography, and created for all time a ''public park or pleasuring ground for the benefit and enjoyment of the people.''

Beautiful America Publishing Company

The nation's foremost publisher of quality color photography

Current Books

Alaska, Arizona, British Columbia, California, California Vol. II, California Coast, California Desert, California Missions, Colorado, Florida, Georgia, Hawaii, Idaho, Las Vegas, Los Angeles, Michigan, Michigan Vol. II, Minnesota, Montana, Montana Vol. II, Mt. Hood (Oregon), New York, New Mexico, Northern California, Northern California Vol. II, North Carolina, North Idaho, Ohio, Oklahoma, Oregon, Oregon Vol. II, Oregon Coast, Oregon Country, Pennsylvania, Pittsburgh, San Diego, San Francisco, San Juan Islands, Seattle, Texas, Utah, Vancouver U.S.A., Virginia, Washington, Washington Vol. II, Washington D.C., Wisconsin, Wyoming, Yosemite National Park

Forthcoming Books

Beauty of Oregon, Beauty of Washington, California Mountains, Chicago, Dallas, Denver, Illinois, Indiana, Kentucky, Maryland, Massachusetts, Mississippi, Missouri, Nevada, New Jersey, New York City, Ozarks, Pacific Coast, Rocky Mountains, South Carolina, Tennessee, Vermont

Large Format, Hardbound Books

Beautiful America, Beauty of California, Glory of Nature's Form, Lewis & Clark Country, Western Impressions

Enlarged Prints

Most of the photography in this book is available as photographic enlargements. Send self-addressed, stamped envelope for information. For a complete product catalog, send $1.00.
Beautiful America Publishing Company
P.O. Box 608
Beaverton, Oregon 97075